Digital Sign Language

Mark Boidman

ACKNOWLEDGMENTS

Thank you to my family and my team at Solomon Partners, including Christian Bermel, Matthew Fryefield, Heidi Heilig, Kalen Holliday, Christian Kasmikha, Blake McCann, Kate Plassman, Trae Smith, Ricky Yoo and Ben Zinder. Thank you to the many Professional Audio Visual and Out of Home Media companies for the insights that helped pull this book together.

Table of Contents

Chapter One

Introduction to Digital Signage

The continued bombardment of 5,000 to 10,000 messages per person, each day across various advertising mediums makes breaking through to consumers and reaching mass audiences increasingly difficult.

Marketing planners and buyers value out of home media (abbreviated as "OOH" and also known as outdoor media) as an effective branding platform. When we were fortunate to advise Netflix on the 2018 acquisition of its Sunset Strip billboard assets, we knew these assets, even as traditional static billboards, would represent one of the most powerful OOH branding platforms in the United States. Leading tech, media and fashion brands are increasingly utilizing eye-catching outdoor print ads highlighting their iconic brand imagery to break through the clutter of a fragmented media market and reach consumers.

What Is Digital Out of Home ("DOOH") Media?

Consider "out of home media" as any form of media that engages with you when you are outside of your home, in contrast to personal forms of media such as your home television or desktop computer. Out of home media is content and advertising delivered on displays that can be found in both public and private environments, including retail stores, hotels, bars, stadiums, elevators, restaurants, fitness centers, malls, airports, on highways and streets, and corporate offices, among various other locations, and can also include mobile phones used in these locations. Media owners are taking their more traditional static offerings on OOH and enhancing them with a digital component to create more advanced DOOH portfolios.

New technology in out of home media provides interactivity and flexibility to these installations, yielding something far more dynamic than traditional outdoor vinyl billboards or printed posters. Today, media launch times are faster and content is streamed across digital networks. Digital technology and hardware costs continue to decrease, making this medium increasingly cost-effective.

What Is Digital Signage?

Digital signage is a form of visual communication using dynamic electronic displays (as opposed to traditional signage, using a static tin/wood/paper display). With the aid of signage, you can more easily achieve your communication goals by which advertising success is measured.

Digital displays use technologies such as LCD, LED, projection and e-paper to display text, digital images, video, web pages, weather data or even restaurant menus. They can be found anywhere people are, and are commonly located in public spaces, transportation systems, museums, stadiums, retail stores, hotels, restaurants and corporate buildings to provide wayfinding, exhibitions, marketing and outdoor advertising. Digital signs are used as a network of electronic displays that are centrally managed and individually addressable for the display of text, animated or video messages for advertising, information, entertainment and merchandising to targeted audiences.

What is Professional AV?

Digital signage is often used as the visual component of professional audiovisual, or Pro AV. Pro AV refers to the high-quality equipment and technicians who work in an event system typically geared to a commercial environment. AV is used to describe electronic media that possesses an audio (sound) and visual (sight) component. The Pro AV industry is a multibillion-dollar industry, made up of manufacturers, dealers, systems integrators, consultants, engineers, programmers, presenters and tech managers of audiovisual products and services.

With greater focus and marketing attention on the physical world of media, the Global Professional Audio Video ("Pro AV") industry is expected to grow to $329 billion in revenue by 2026.

Global Professional Audio Video ("AV") Revenue ($ in Billions)[1]

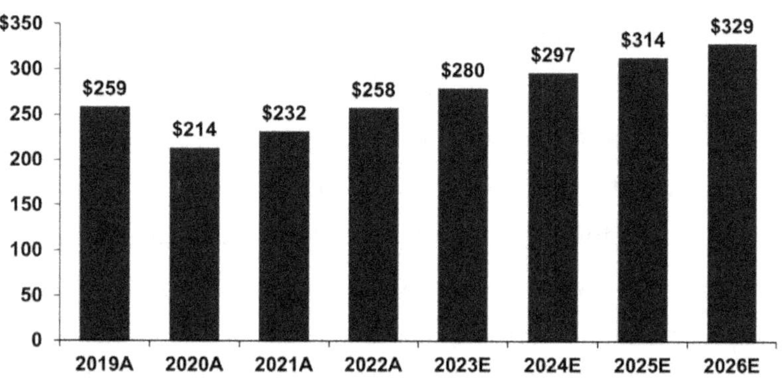

The global Pro AV market is categorized into commercial, education, government, hospitality and other market subsectors. Among these, the education subsector accounts for one of the largest markets, massively boosted during the COVID- 19 pandemic, along with rapid urbanization across the globe. Pro AV is widely used for smart learning systems in schools, universities, and various academic and research institutions. For example, the use of multi-touch high-definition

---

[1] Avixa AV Industry Outlook and Trends Analysis (IOTA) Global.

(HD) televisions (TVs) enhances real-time blended teaching and learning by augmenting creative visualization for improved classroom experience.

Pro AV is also being installed in retail stores, transit stations, shopping centers, exhibition halls, hotels and stadiums to attract consumers' attention and influence consumers' buying decisions, driving Pro AV market growth.

Professional audio, sometimes abbreviated as pro audio, refers to both an activity and a category of high quality, studio-grade audio equipment. When professionally combined with a visual component, such as digital signage, it transforms an experience or message into a feeling and a memory. Typically, it encompasses sound recording, sound reinforcement system setup, audio mixing, and studio music production by trained sound and audio engineers, record producers, graphics designers and programmers.

Advancements in high-definition display technologies are changing the way Pro AV equipment is being used to communicate, broadcast, interact, collaborate and advertise in commercial environments. This has enabled higher performance, flexibility and scalability to the Pro AV industry.

Chapter Two

Pro AV Industry Trends

Industries that require large physical gatherings were hit especially hard in 2020, however all Pro AV subsectors are expected to grow in the future. Cinema and Venues / Events declined more than 40% in 2020 but are expected to grow the fastest in 2023.

Industries ranked by Pro AV market revenue, largest to smallest, are as follows:

1. Corporate
2. Venues / Events
3. Media / Entertainment
4. Education
5. Retail
6. Government / Military
7. Residential
8. Hospitality

9. Transportation

10. Energy

11. Healthcare

12. Cinema

<u>Total Pro AV Market Revenue By Industry</u>[2]

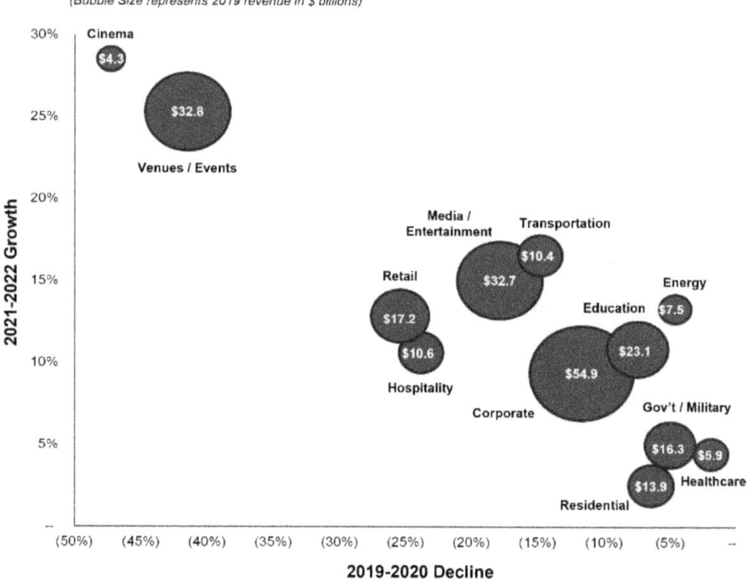

---

[2] AVIXA.

Pro AV Use Cases

<u>Retail</u>

Retailers are increasingly using personalized, user-friendly, interactive, and touchless displays to create engaging ways to reach customers and drive foot traffic to their stores, with Pro AV displays in particular used to elevate in-store experiences through unique sensory experiences.

Storefronts, which represent a marketing opportunity for retailers, are being upgraded with customized installations for visitors to enjoy and enhance the consumer experience.

Interactivity is further improving the experience by combining real-time face capture and projection mapping that can overlay videos onto surfaces, including walls and buildings.

Retailers can show relevant messaging on digital screens, instantly displaying timely information to create helpful signage for customers that can easily adapt to a store's changing needs. Important store updates and marketing opportunities, such as flash sales, open hours and high-demand product availability, constitute just some of the information that retailers use to reach consumers.

In addition, wayfinding signage can help customers easily navigate retail environments.

In order to create one-of-a-kind experiences, retailers can now put together temporary "pop-up" experiences, which create "Instagrammable" content in retail environments. These experiences have become one of the fastest-growing social media marketing strategies and offer a way for retailers to access younger audiences.

Projector displays are excellent for creating "retailtainment" opportunities given their easy installation and flexible display options.

Through all these display formats, technology differentiates venues, drawing in traffic and driving revenue using location-based targeted ads with in-store promotions. The success of these advertisements can be monitored using device ID metrics, impression multipliers, and the retailers own purchase data to provide real time analytics for retailers to assess the success of their campaigns.

<u>Smart Cities</u>

A smart city is one in which services within the city, and products that are delivered within the city, are connected by the internet. Smart Cities can ensure optimum utilization and allocation of resources, which can help improve a geographical area's economy in the long run. Because of this interconnected network, city services such as trash collection, street lighting and parking meters can operate more efficiently and with less human intervention. Automating many of these services reduces fuel consumption and lessens vehicle wear and tear. This also has the added benefit of redirecting employee focus toward enhancing the safety of the community.

Some advantages of Smart Cities include:

- Trash containers can indicate when they are almost full, reducing the frequency of collection
- Streetlights can detect when it is raining during the day, and automatically turn on for public safety
- Parking meters can alert people when their time is running low, improving the consumer shopping and dining experience.

The ever-increasing demand and concern for public safety, economic growth, government urbanization initiatives and efficient communication have emphasized the need for Smart Cities. The global Smart City market is expected to grow to $1,024 billion by the year 2026, with a 4-year CAGR of 14.9%.[3]

Other sources indicate that Smart Cities represent a $1.5 trillion market opportunity.[4] Based on current trends, it appears to be much larger than that. The $1.5 trillion figure includes not just

---

[3] Planet Crust.
[4] Forbes.

digital signage or media, it also includes energy, transportation, infrastructure, and governance, as well as technology. Many of these services will be paid for by media and advertising.

In New York, London and other parts of the United Kingdom, cities are beginning to roll out free, public Wi-Fi networks. These networks are secure and safe for the public, as well as for city services and vendors. City vendors can integrate with city services within the Wi-Fi network to provide what is called "connected city services."

Right now, it is estimated that there are more than 250 Smart City projects in 178 cities worldwide. According to a recent study, out of the remaining cities that had not employed Smart City software, 25% were considering implementing some sort of Smart City software solution in the future. One way that areas, including New York City, have supported the cost associated with free Wi-Fi in a connected network is through advertising.

Retail intersects seamlessly within Smart Cities. As cities get smarter, retail stores in these cities can connect to the network as well, which can shape how consumers shop. In fact, you may see a situation in which a screen on the outside of a shop window becomes the store. The consumer can use touch-screen technology to make their purchases right then and there. An example of this is an interactive touch screen 'storefront'. Interactive touch screen storefronts are innovative retail displays that allow customers to engage with products and services through intuitive touch-based interfaces.

Consumers could also shop on screens in subway stations and have the products delivered to their home, possibly that same day. Even vending machines are becoming interactive, designed to provide media content, advertising and purchase content. These touch screens are created to feel like giant tablets or iPads which makes the new experience comfortable and intuitive for consumers.

Workplace

Building automation via the hardware and software that is being added to commercial buildings, especially in office spaces, continues to be a major trend. Implementation of commercial building Pro AV technology can boost engagement and efficiency in a workplace, resulting in greater profitability.

<u>AV Technology Becoming Further Integrated Within Workplaces[5]</u>

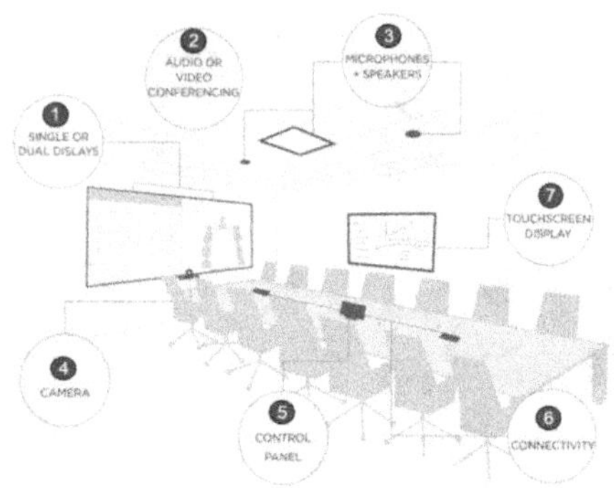

1 Single / Dual Displays

- Large, high-definition displays enable colleagues to see each other during video-calls
- Displays used for screen sharing / presenting

2 Audio / Video Conferencing

- Conference rooms are equipped with Zoom, Microsoft Teams or other platforms to enable communication with remote colleagues and clients

3 Microphone / Speakers

- High-quality microphone / speakers and correct installation—in ceiling, on-table, or sound bar below the display—have a significant impact on the conference room experience

4 Camera

- Rooms staged for video conferencing require a camera, which is typically situated under the display so teams can view the display and appear in the frame at the same time

5 Control Panel

- Functions as the control center for the audiovisual system in the room
- User interface is critical for creating a seamless experience

6 Connectivity

- Wireless, wired, or a combination of wired and wireless connectivity enable screensharing, video conferencing and presenting

7 Touchscreen Display

- Interactive whiteboards are valuable tools for collaboration
- Some video conferencing platforms enable whiteboard screen sharing

---

[5] Source: Solomon Partners.

Conference rooms can be equipped with user-friendly audiovisual technology to create a seamless hybrid work environment. Using large, high-definition single and dual displays enables colleagues to see each other during video-calls. These displays can be used for screen sharing, presenting, and audiovisual conferencing.

In addition, conference rooms are equipped with software application platforms to enable communication with remote colleagues and clients.

High-quality microphones and speakers installed in the ceiling, on the table or with the sound bar below the display have a significant impact on the conference room experience.

Wired and wireless connectivity enable screensharing, video conferencing, and presenting that mimics the fully in-person experience with its level of simplicity.

Rooms staged for video conferencing also require a camera, which is typically situated under the display, allowing call participants to view discussion materials on screen and appear in the frame at the same time as they would during a more traditional in-person gathering.

Many office set-ups also have a control panel that functions as the operating center for the audiovisual system in the room. This user interface is critical for creating a seamless experience where someone in the room has full control of a meeting process.

Additionally, interactive whiteboards used as touchscreen displays are valuable tools for collaboration. There are certain video conferencing platforms that enable whiteboard screen sharing.

The office environment can now be more fully controlled – including displays, lights, shades and audio – and hybrid meetings are being held seamlessly under one Pro AV ecosystem.

Virtual Reception

Smart virtual receptionist devices can also increase building efficiency by helping to control visitor traffic flow and room occupancy, leading occupants to rooms and seats that have been sanitized or unused and provide a solution for contact tracing.

A virtual receptionist is an excellent choice if your company is scaling up and needs scalable administrative solutions quickly. Smart virtual receptionist devices are increasingly more common in new buildings. Lobby technology, including virtual receptionists and digital signage, is expected to make buildings more efficient given the data that is aggregated by such technology.

Vehicle Media

Signage on or inside of vehicles, including ride-sharing vehicles, creates an additional revenue stream for drivers and ride-sharing vehicle operating companies. Exterior signs can be seen by pedestrians and other drivers, while digital screens inside the vehicle can support advertising, accessibility, provide entertainment, gather passenger information via surveys or simplify the payment process. We believe that certain types of vehicle media and advertising will continue to expand beyond urban centers and become increasingly common among ride-sharing transit generally.

We believe the use cases for Pro AV technology are broad and encounter the consumer at all stages of their day. Whether on the commute to or from work, in the workplace itself or when off the clock, audio-visual technology is influencing modern experience in a meaningful way.

2023 Pro AV Trends

Physical spaces and events with scale are being designed with an emphasis on audiovisual technology to enhance the visitor experience.

Video Walls / Visual Explosions

Spaces requiring video displays will increasingly opt for video walls over projection screens, as video wall costs continue to decrease and technology outpaces traditional project screens.

Visual explosions and other highly eye-catching content on video walls are other effective ways to capture people's attention as companies push the boundaries of what is possible through digital media.

Live Streaming

Live streaming events from home has become commonplace and comfortable in the wake of hybrid work environments and expanding virtual access. As the world continues to embrace live streaming, businesses increasingly need equipment that aids streaming, including sophisticated production systems, cameras and microphones.

QR Codes

Consumers are increasingly expecting convenient, personal, touchless interaction and information. The ability to remain contactless and provide new opportunities for advertisers to reach consumers with profitable displays and touchless purchases is critical to the Pro AV sector. Other interactive displays rely on apps and non-touch screens for activation. A recent study conducted by eMarketer found that the number of smartphone users in the United States (18+) who use QR codes is accelerating and projected to reach nearly 100 million by 2025.

U.S. Smartphone QR Code Users (18+)[6]

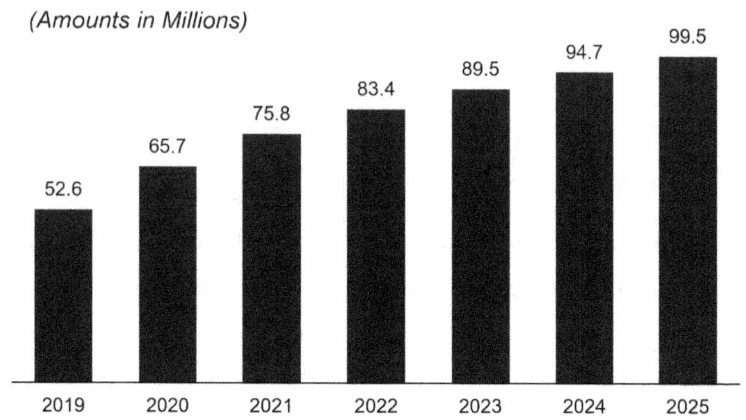

Virtual Green Screens

As events and conferences continue to go virtual or hybrid, green screens will continue to be used as a backdrop for speakers. High quality green screens are a simple way to enhance the viewing experience by creating more enticing backgrounds and a cost-effective way to insert branding and infographics.

Pro AV combines virtual green screens with branding and infographics inserted virtually on the background screen behind off-site presenters to enhance the viewer's experience, create a

---

[6] eMarketer.

more professional presentation, and generate a feeling that the presenter is on-site and more readily available to help them.

Virtual green screen software makes cutting-edge background removal and blurring possible without the need for a physical green screen. In addition, virtual green screens combine easily with most streaming software.

Market Expansion and Technological Innovations

<u>Touchless Solutions</u>

New technologies offering touchless solutions include voice control and gesture commands.

The amplified focus on sanitation will continue to increase demand for touchless interactivity. Studies have shown that most individuals find communal touchscreens unhygienic and prefer touchless solutions.

<u>Integrated Mobile Experience</u>

Digital signage will be further integrated with mobile devices, allowing users to control signage displays by altering the display's content themselves through their mobile devices.

Restaurants are actively replacing physical menus with digital signage and QR codes, allowing customers to access menus from their own devices rather than touching a shared menu. Menu updates in this case also do not require reprinting and thus reduce waste and carbon footprint impact.

Retail stores also use QR codes to enable visitors to scan items and read customer review information on their mobile devices, saving employees time and providing customers more transparency on the products available for purchase.

The future of advertising will carefully focus on where the consumer has been, where the consumer is and what the consumer may do next. The goal here is to develop consumer patterns in the form of a predictive algorithm. This is not the future of personalized advertising – this is or should be advertising today. If you are thinking that this sounds like a scene from Steven Spielberg's 2002 sci-fi thriller, *Minority Report*, you are not far off base. In one frequently cited scene,

Tom Cruise walks through a shopping mall and an iris code is used to trigger digital media displays of advertisements based on his mental state and context.

There are multiple examples of out of home companies we know well today using facial recognition and other identifying technology coupled with digital signage and/or a network of screens that can adapt content based on gender and age. Retargeting in this sense adds the benefit of being able to anticipate customer needs before such needs are even outwardly expressed. By understanding the needs and movements of your audience, mobile content can be optimized and delivered at the precise time and place it is desired.

Digital Communications Displays

Immersive digital signage has become a necessity in public venues, as opposed to a rare sight reserved for more upscale areas. Digital signage can be used to communicate important site updates in real time and offers interactive wayfinding. Examples of digital communication displays include digital directories at mall locations, digital transit schedules and in-store digital kiosks.

Advertising

Digital signage allows advertisers to deliver targeted messages and update or change content in a matter of seconds. Using AI, these messages or advertisements have become programmatic with automatic advertising purchases when buyer conditions are met for granular targeting.

Though consumers are increasingly engaging with digital out of home media and digital signage at "eye-level" and in-venue (e.g., restaurants, transit stops, medical waiting rooms, etc.), there is real opportunity to engage with millions of people using "spectacular" billboards in locations with high dwell time. These billboards are increasingly engaging consumers through the use of social media, gaming, photo sharing, digital commerce, and retargeting integrations. Spectacular billboards are among the largest digital signage displays in use today. Generally found in heavily pedestrian trafficked locations such as Times Square, Sunset Boulevard or the Las Vegas Strip, these truly unique displays often incorporate special effects as well. As advisors to media companies, we have been actively raising this underused media opportunity to various diversified media and retail companies as an important medium to break through the clutter to reach their consumers.

There is no question that the future of digital media is the ability to connect with consumers who want fulfillment that is both instantaneous and personalized. Companies with digital platforms that continue to focus on consumer and mobile interaction will be rewarded through increased customer engagement. The more iconic the media location (e.g., the spectacular billboards in Times Square), the better able the signage is to engage consumers with cutting-edge technology.

As people are increasingly mobile, it is important to understand new technologies and the impact of video and digital signage on our physical world and related opportunities for investors.

Chapter Three

The Power of Digital Signage

Digital Signage is a Visual Medium

The human brain responds quickly and efficiently to well-crafted information presented on screens.

According to the University of Minnesota Carlson School of Management, presentations that use visual aids are 43% more persuasive than those that do not, and digital signage increases brand awareness by 48%. The consumer finds information received visually to be more persuasive (think of the old adage "seeing is believing"). This can present challenges with artificial intelligence and augmented reality where media in the physical world will prove to be increasingly authentic and "real."

Digital signage is visual, which makes it easier for viewers to digest and remember information and feel comfortable that it is real if located in an authoritative environment. It makes it easy to engage and recognize achievements, to communicate an organization's brand and values, and to persuade people to follow a call to action or make a purchase.

Statistically 52% of Americans say they've seen a digital sign in the past week. Of those, 47% remember seeing a specific ad or message, and recall jumps to 55% when talking about outdoor digital billboards.[7]

---

[7] Visix.

Advertising Effectiveness – Solomon Partners Study and Recall Comparison Analysis[8]

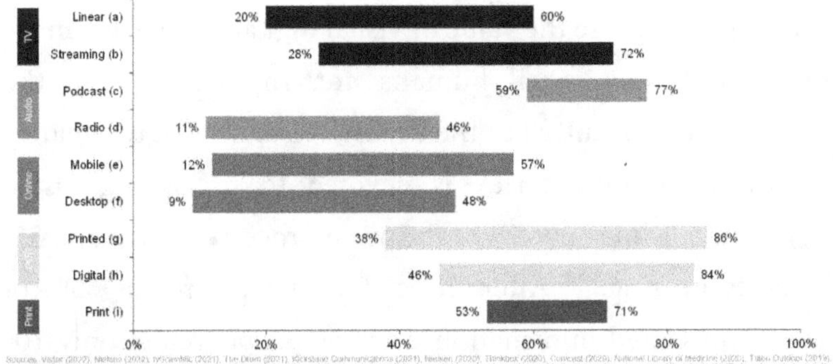

Regarding retail digital signage, 80% of shoppers say they have entered a store because a digital sign caught their interest. Studies indicate that 59% of people who see digital signage want to learn more about the topic.[9] 19% of viewers made an unplanned purchase of something promoted digitally in a retail setting, and in restaurants, the number of unplanned purchases after viewing digital advertising jumped to 80%.[10] In a recent study, 4 out of 5 brands noticed a 33% increase in sales after

---

[8] Solomon Partners.

[9] Mvix.

[10] Mvix.

adopting digital signage.[11] Even adding a single on-premise sign adds an average of 4.75% in annual sales revenue.[12]

It's easy to recognize the value of visual digital signage when we think about how visual humans are. In fact, 90% of the information transmitted to the brain is visual.[13] Approximately 30% of the brain's cortex is devoted to processing visual information, while only 8% of the brain processes touch and 3% processes hearing. [14] After three days, people retain 65% of visually presented information whereas people retain only 10-20% of written or spoken information after three days.[15] Our brains process visual information 60,000x faster than text.[16] It's no wonder presentations that use visual aids are 43% more persuasive than those that don't.[17]

The Bull Case for Digital Out of Home Advertising

Recent changes put OOH, including digital out of home (DOOH), at the forefront of valuable branding platforms. Security and privacy changes in Apple's operating system software that limit targeted digital advertising will result in the

---

[11] Screenfluence.

[12] Fit1Media.

[13] Visual Teaching Alliance.

[14] Seyens.

[15] Changing Minds.

[16] International Forum of Visual Practitioners.

[17] Ethos3.

democratization of targeting and measurement across advertising channels, with ad dollars shifting into the OOH funnel as a result.

The rise of digital billboard and other digital OOH solutions has enabled the outdoor advertising market to grow steadily. Even as traditional media has lost market share, the outdoor advertising market has expanded. Moreover, outdoor advertising has been crucial in reaching young urbanites as TV viewing time for young adults continues to decline. Outdoor advertising represents an opportunity to reach this audience without the ad blocking and false impressions issues inherent in online or other new media advertising. Within outdoor advertising, top media and tech companies consistently outspend other companies relative to their ad budgets. In fact, outdoor media allocation for leading media and tech companies exceeds the average outdoor spend by the top 100 advertisers.

Solomon Partners Analysis on Select Media and Tech Companies[18]

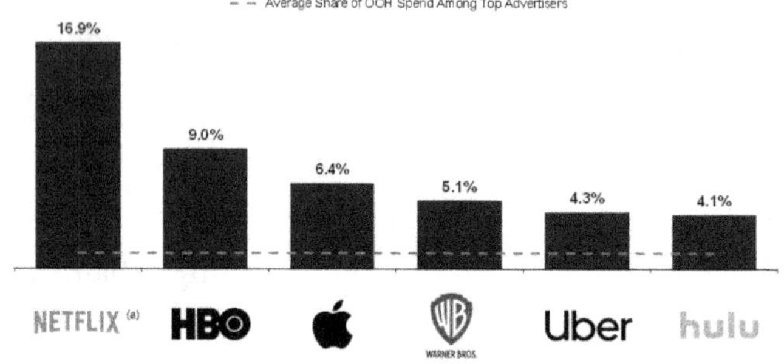

Programmatic Advertising and Other Growth Opportunities

Programmatic buying provides a key opportunity for outdoor advertising to increase its share of media spend. Media advertising has traditionally been a negotiated affair, where ad agencies serve as the middlemen between brands and operators, and traditional ad buying restricts brands to contracts that run a predetermined number of ads with a publisher. Programmatic buying is a way for buyers and sellers to find deals based on specific audience requirements. Choices might include number

---

[18] Solomon Partners, OAAA 2021 Megabrands report.
[a] Netflix data as of 2018.

of impressions, audience demographics, geography, weather patterns and more.

Once the right audience becomes available, the purchase is made automatically without human interaction. For example, a billboard in a subway station could make its advertising more contextually relevant based on the type of commuters traveling at certain times. Coffee shops could showcase coffee or breakfast goods advertising during consumers' morning commute and bars or restaurants could do the same during consumers' evening commute.

With programmatic buying, algorithms are used to automate the buying, placement and optimization of media inventory through a real time bidding system. Data analytics also provide brands with metrics on campaign effectiveness, which allows them to make real time adjustments.

Whereas in the past, signage was only a set placement over a set duration of time. The ability to provide granular reporting has enhanced the value media owners are able to create for clients using out of home campaigns.

Another reason programmatic buying is an opportunity within OOH is due to the significant room for growth within the industry, as less than half of media planners today understand that OOH advertising can be purchased programmatically, and even fewer currently think of programmatic as the default way to transact.

Solomon Partners Programmatic Buying Graph[19]

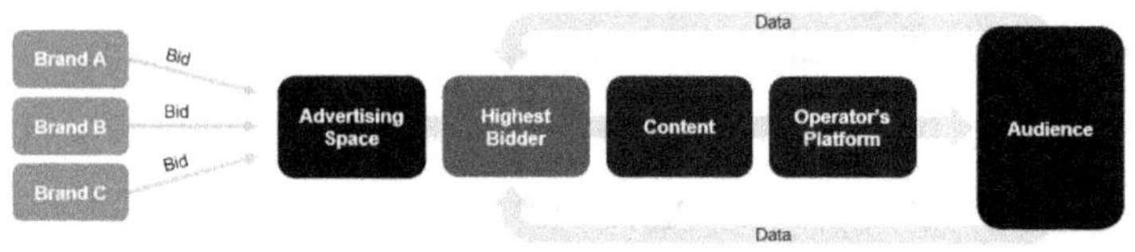

Operators are also developing programmatic platforms to integrate OOH media with mobile and online sources, allowing buyers to purchase multi-screen campaigns to help media owners reach previously inaccessible markets.

The digital out of home sector is unique within the broader digital programmatic ecosystem. When looking at the digital ecosystem, you see many supply side platforms that plug into millions of partners, all of them individually. In the DOOH sector, you have only a few scaled supply inventory partners.

---

[19] Screemedia, eMarketer, OAAA, MediaPost, DPAA and Digital Signage Pulse.

<u>U.S. OOH Media Model – Solomon Partners Breakdown[20]</u>

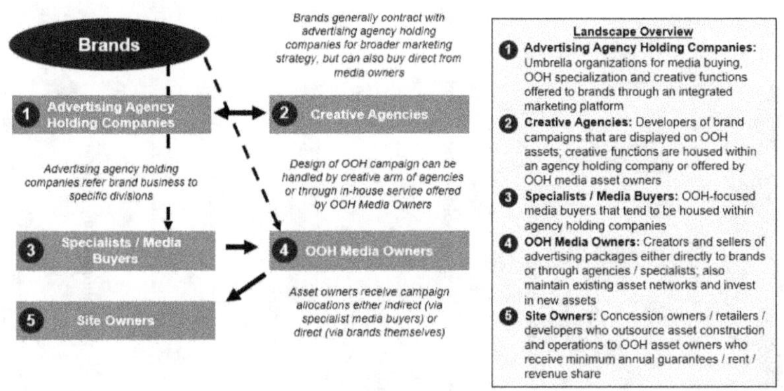

Other growth and income opportunities for OOH companies are the utilization of digital conversions, expansion into new geographic markets and to grow screen count. Again, utilizing programmatic sales to reduce campaign friction and improve profit is an opportunity worth pursuing.

---

[20] Solomon Partners.

Key Equity Value Creation Factors for OOH Owners[21]

	Commentary
Organic Revenue Growth 	▪ Path for expansion despite broader macroeconomic factors around availability of M&A targets ▪ Need to prove (i) ability to grow / expand location base absent M&A and/or (ii) ability to grow rate or occupancy / utilization over the medium- to long-term
Proven ROI 	▪ Ability to prove out ROI attracts brands that prioritize quantitative data ▪ Can drive CPM growth if ads are currently underpriced vs. measured return
Ability to Effectively Execute M&A 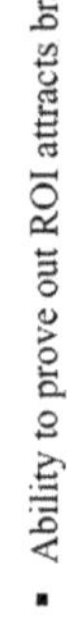	▪ High value-add if management can identify and acquire assets currently under-sold by the market ▪ Provides a path to growth even through an economic downturn ▪ Sponsors look for opportunities for multiple arbitrage on smaller targets ▪ Good teams can also capitalize on cost synergies
Capex Dynamics 	▪ High ROI on new builds demonstrates strong fundamental unit economics ▪ Strong payback periods on new device rollout is a key metric ▪ Burden of capital expenditure installations – more favorable from a FCF perspective if building owner pays for capex
Footprint / Scale 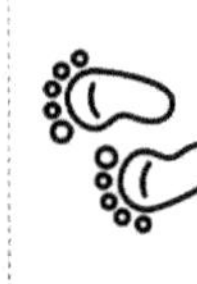	▪ Larger footprints attract larger, national advertising accounts – Ad agencies typically require substantial scale before showing interest in platform ▪ Meaningful operating leverage within scaled platforms ▪ Geographical diversity within footprint provides for superior cash flow risk profile

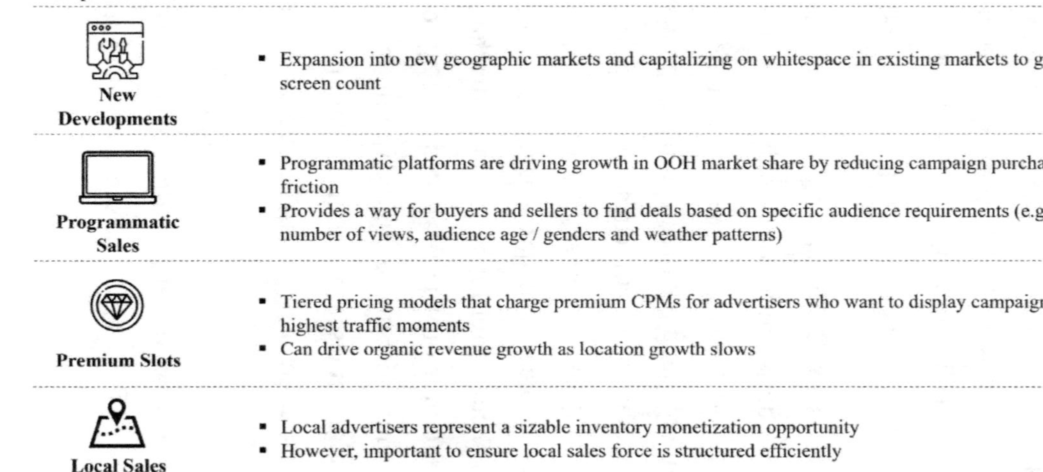

	Commentary
Digital Conversions	• Digital conversions generally drive 4x – 6x revenue increases with little incremental cost • Typically high capex requirements, but payback periods tend to be short and costs continue to decrease
Attribution Improvements	• Technology improvements that increase attribution capabilities make ROI more measurable and enable operators to charge clients premium CPMs
New Developments	• Expansion into new geographic markets and capitalizing on whitespace in existing markets to grow screen count
Programmatic Sales	• Programmatic platforms are driving growth in OOH market share by reducing campaign purchasing friction • Provides a way for buyers and sellers to find deals based on specific audience requirements (e.g., number of views, audience age / genders and weather patterns)
Premium Slots	• Tiered pricing models that charge premium CPMs for advertisers who want to display campaigns at highest traffic moments • Can drive organic revenue growth as location growth slows
Local Sales	• Local advertisers represent a sizable inventory monetization opportunity • However, important to ensure local sales force is structured efficiently

[21] Solomon Partners.

Transit Media

OOH advertising in the transit space has enjoyed strong growth over the last decade. Experts anticipate this to remain an exceptionally strong sub-sector of OOH.

The reason behind transit's success in the OOH market is the opportunity to convert millions of static boards into digital signs. Transit networks do not typically require permits to convert static signage to digital which restricts the amount of digital signage in more regulated areas. In addition, signage on commercial businesses and ride-sharing vehicles creates a new revenue stream for the drivers or businesses, as well as an opportunity for advertisers. Data shows that the transit category accounts for $1.1 billion in ad spending but that digital accounts for just $140 million.[22] Digital assets have performed well in a short time in operation and experts are forecasting even stronger demand and related growth in the coming years.

Historically transit contracts generally carried five- or ten-year terms between the OOH operators and the municipalities. A number of contracts will be up for renewal, which will serve as a catalyst for future negotiations to switch from static to digital advertising.

---

[22] Delta Media.

Pedestrian Level Signage

Historically, the focus on digital OOH advertising has been on massive billboards on major roadways; however, pedestrian-level signage offers a more personal, eye-level connection with consumers. The opportunity in this sub-sector lies in the consumer's proximity to each display. Pedestrian-level signage is street-level, offering consumers the ability to engage with the signage as they walk by.

These displays represent the comfort point between a consumer's personal in-home devices (cell phones, tablets) and the larger-than-life, excitement of large-format digital billboards.

Smaller businesses are grabbing the attention of 'experience' purchasers with pedestrian-level signage on storefronts, urban walking paths and pop-up experiences. While these experiences might be slightly less memorable than larger format signage, the friendly feel of digital pedestrian-level signage adds dwell time keeping consumers in place longer.

The creative use of pedestrian-level outdoor advertising is evolving. Where previously six words were considered the minimum, one word can be enough when combined with visuals. Used with evocative or provocative photography, smaller brands can elevate their stature. Outdoor LED posters can even accommodate 3D effects and animations, creating eye-catching visuals. Social media and artificial intelligence makes it hard to tell the difference between what is real and what is not, but pedestrian-level digital posters are a welcoming real-world presence that builds trust and credibility.

Innovation in Digital Signage

Spaces and events are increasingly being designed with an emphasis on immersive digital signage and audiovisual technology to enhance the visitor / customer experience. Advertisers and sponsors use digital signage to reach consumers in a way that almost replicates an in-person conversation.

Historically, there have been three generations of digital signage. The first generation was simple dot matrix displays with information having to be input manually, and completely unable to play multimedia content. The second generation was able to utilize multimedia components. The third generation, where we are today, added the function of interactive digital signage and the ability to change content immediately and in real time.

Looking at the brick-and-mortar retail store, we can see that the importance of getting customers the products they need and giving them a great experience to keep them coming back is a constant imperative. However, physical stores must constantly devise new methods to attract consumers and their attention in an increasingly fragmented media and marketing world. Today, the brick-and-mortar store of the future will need to hit the innovation button to create an experience that will level the playing field with the online in-home shopping 'store'.

Knowing that they may be unable to compete on price or breadth of inventory, many brick-and-mortar retailers know they must compete on experience instead.

Already, retailers have been adopting new innovations, including touchscreens to facilitate checkout, apps to help find products in the store, and digital displays to keep customers up to date on both in-store product features and safety measures.

Using digital signage, retail leaders can brace for supply challenges using innovative technology, embrace the retailtainment model for shoppers who want more than just goods and services, and be ready to deliver products more efficiently through multiple channels.

The retailers who want to engage customers will continue to embrace new strategies to enhance the in-store experience. Retailers will also focus on providing customers a great atmosphere, delivering excellent customer service, offering personalized experiences, connecting customers with the right product or service and providing a frictionless experience overall. Ultimately, continued customer engagement depends upon creating a great in-store experience that makes customers want to return and have the fun, out-and-about experience. The draw is all about the hybrid of a digital and physical experience.

The future of digital signage will be all about asking: What is the purpose of a physical space and what can it serve? Who is the audience? What kind of experience do we want the specific audience to have?

Decision makers not only need to be thinking in terms of the 'wow' factor, but also what value the interactive signage will actually add to the physical location.

Going forward toward new innovations, it is important to avoid the common mistake of thinking only at the beginning about content strategy. While it is a good idea to know what you will put on the screen as initial content, you will need to consider what will be on the screen tomorrow, next month and next year. Content can become stale if not refreshed, or prohibitively expensive if refreshed frequently without adequate planning.

A building lobby's captivating video wall should provides a beautiful experience, but it should not provide the same experience every day. So how can a business make its digital signage experience more dynamic? There are 'wow' moments, but you need something else to fill the space and not become just a high-end screensaver.

A place where melding the 'wow' factor with productive or practical interactive information will be essential is the travel industry. Businesses within the industry will need to use Pro AV and digital OOH to excite travelers about their destination, providing them a moment of surprise and delight, while at the same time using practical elements of wayfinding.

Digital signage content creators should focus on how they can use the digital experience to solve a problem, or build on, reinforce and magnify a good experience.

Finally, to encourage innovation, businesses can bring in Pro AV integrators earlier in the process to help new experiential design be built into their spaces. We'll discuss Pro AV integrators further in Chapter 5.

Chapter Four

Digital Signage on Premise

OOH is a superior channel for contextual engagement as it is place-based. Physical DOOH networks correlate with specific places and audiences.

For example, fitness center screens target 'Generation Active,' while office elevator screens target professionals.

What Is On-Premise Media?

On-premise tech refers to hardware infrastructure and software deployed and running within the physical location of an organization. On-premise infrastructure is the software and technology that is located within the physical confines of an enterprise, often in the company's data center as opposed to running remotely. In on-premise systems, the data stays in the organization's private network, granting the organization complete control over such infrastructure.

On-premise media allows advertisers to reach the right consumers at the right time in venues. Through the use of new technologies and measurement capabilities, companies can optimize their advertising efforts by focusing on the precise audience each company wants to reach as opposed to a broader channel through which they may be able to reach them. Within OOH specifically, programmatic advertising platforms are driving growth in OOH market share, as well as on-premise media, by reducing campaign purchase friction significantly.

DOOH Innovating the On-Premise Landscape[23]

Data-driven content on DOOH screens also provides greater engagement, stronger delivery and **increased retention** to advertising campaigns

Campaigns are transitioning from linear content (simple movie files) to contextual, **interactive and dynamic displays**

Sensors now advanced enough to react to **external stimuli** and evolve on-screen messages; inputs include temperature, views, precipitation and wind speed

DOOH screens are also able to respond to **real-time data**, such as pricing changes, location, audience demographics, weather and time of day

These platforms allow buyers and sellers to find deals based on specific audience requirements (e.g., number of views, audience

---

[23] Source: Solomon Partners.

age / genders and weather patterns). Once the right audience becomes available, the purchase is made automatically without any human or media specialist interaction.

Businesses have more control of on-premise IT assets by maintaining their performance, security and upkeep, as well as the physical location. For example, many legacy and traditional data center resources exist on-premise. Since the licensee runs the software in their own data center on their own or rented hardware, this is also called "in-house". In contrast to cloud computing, customers of on-premise models have full control over data, but also assume responsibility for the associated risks. Use of the provider's hardware is not possible with on-premise signage.

<u>Video in the Physical World</u>

Due to tremendous strides made by filmmaking and technology industries in accessibility and production capability, to the point where even mobile phones are capable of shooting feature length films, the public has become accustomed to feeling connected through digital means. All forms of video technology are ripe for creative development. Advertisers can now take an out of home campaign and make it work well with display, mobile or other digital channels.

Video works across sports and entertainment organizations, but also larger brands, museums, retail and entertainment, including theme parks and malls.

DOOH should encompass on-premise media to account for the fact that video / digital signage growth in the physical world is exploding. The $8-9 billion of U.S. ad spend that is traditionally reserved for OOH is poised to grow significantly, primarily due to re-allocation of spending from other media channels, including over-the-top (OTT), online video and mobile.

Growing Role of Mobile

<u>Digital Signage and Location-Based Mobile Technology[24]</u>

The combination of **digital signage** displays with **location-based mobile technology** provides advertisers with multiple points of entry to a prospective consumer

Consumers are more likely to go online via mobile device for social media, web searching and shopping within **30 minutes** of seeing an outdoor / OOH advertisement	Advertisers are beginning to recognize additional **flexibility** and relevance that digital platforms provide	Combining placement and timing has the potential to **amplify** and extend brand engagement to unprecedented levels

---

[24] Source: Solomon Partners.

Geolocation technology is a massive game changer that is revolutionizing our physical world with personalized digital media and digital/mobile commerce. GPS-enabled smartphones are everywhere, and nothing will stop geolocation, not even privacy concerns. Imagine having checked in for a connecting flight and the airline closes its door to the aircraft a moment before you arrive at the gate. Now think about what geolocation technology can do to change the outcome. It is only a matter of time before your airline tracks and knows your exact location and holds the door open a moment longer or knows that you are too far away and decides to more efficiently pull away from the gate moments earlier than its planned departure. Or perhaps the screens in the airport lounges only come on and stay on when you are physically in or approaching the lounge. Or the specific content displayed on the screen in the lounge welcomes you by name as a frequent flier/customer.

Geolocation and indoor positioning system technology are also bridging the physical world to digital/mobile commerce. In the quick service restaurant sector, for example, consumers are increasingly ordering via a mobile device that provides them with a method of ordering and higher level of engagement.

Quick service restaurants are also experimenting with location-based services to alert restaurant employees when consumers are within a geo-fenced area around the store, which triggers an order placed via mobile app to be freshly prepared for the customer. Quick service restaurants can use this technology to gain better control over their customers and the customer experience.

Out of home media can be a gateway to retargeting, which is a form of targeted advertising based on a customer's previous behavior. Contextually relevant out of home media content, coupled with geolocation and consumer behavior data, provide a unique opportunity to retarget viewers with behaviorally triggered mobile communications, including advertisements. There have been a few companies that develop table-side tablets for restaurants and bars and these tablets could serve as an out of home retargeting platform to maximize future engagement and conversion.

One example of out of home media content that is contextually relevant to the location would be a table-side tablet promoting a drink special with Hershey's chocolate syrup. When the consumer buys the drink special, whether or not he pays with his mobile phone, data is captured, and the next day, as the consumer approaches a supermarket, he receives an offer for Hershey's chocolate syrup, or potentially another brand of chocolate syrup. This form of media and advertising retargeting is efficient and trackable, especially as mobile technology has the ability to capture the complete path to purchase, including at the physical cash register with PayPal, Square, and others. These use cases translate into incremental advertising spend given the proven uplift in conversion and ROI.

Today, there are multiple examples of out of home companies using facial recognition and other technology, coupled with digital signage and/or a network of screens that can adapt content based on gender and age. Retargeting adds the benefit of being able to anticipate customer needs before such needs are even expressed. By understanding the needs and movements of your audience, mobile content can be optimized and delivered at the precise time and place. It is these types of technologies that cause digitally connected consumers to increasingly want and expect digital engagement everywhere. Even a home shower can now be controlled digitally. And consumer data from intelligent signage and other systems, in-store or in-venue, is being used to increase sales and improve the customer experience and engagement. Fortunately, no one is collecting data on your home showering behaviors (that I know of). Digitally connected consumers and mobile technology provide out of home media companies with a new ability to track an audience and its behavior and should work with existing forms of out of home media measurement.

One of the principal causes driving the steady growth of OOH is the fact that mobile phones have been a real accelerator of growth. People are more mobile and on-the-go than ever before.

The more mobilization pervades society, the greater the opportunity becomes to connect with the consumer closer to the point of sale.

Out of home will also benefit from a relative standpoint, as other media channels have difficulty adapting to technology. Since technology isn't always as much of a friend to other forms of advertising as it is in the OOH industry, over time, this will benefit out of home, whereas other forms of media such as newspapers may struggle. For example, as seen in the chart below, legacy forms of media such as audio/radio and publishing/newspapers are losing advertising dollars as consumers gain more control over the content in front of them, while out of home has remained a mainstay of advertisers' focus and spend in a mobile society.

Ad Spending YoY Growth by Medium[25]

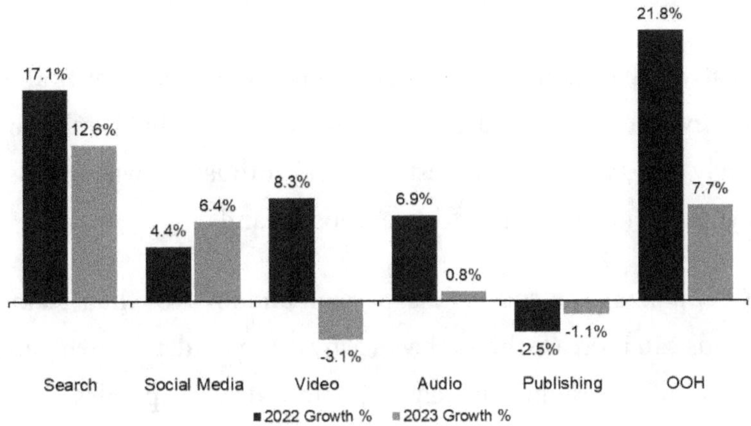

Digital Signage and Sports

Dynamic entertainment districts and arenas can add value and importance to communities and improve brand awareness by delivering timely information about products, services, public service and sports news. It takes only seconds to be inspired by key Olympic and sports moments broadcast instantaneously on DOOH billboards.

Inside and outside sports stadiums, large format digital displays make a huge impact, as surprise and delight moments during a

---

[25] Sources: Consolidated 2023 US ad forecast reports from Dentsu, GroupM, Zenith and 2023 Magna US ad spend forecast report.

game are captured, displayed and explode on social media where the views are immediately shared.

Creative advertising strategies are being implemented by brands to deliver context-based, timely content in a way that is relevant, timely and sparks the interest of sports enthusiasts who are also paying attention to the efforts of those brands.

By capitalizing on sports fans' passion and love for their teams, brands can increase their relevance by using bold, pertinent, and impactful messaging, which ultimately drives up sales. Even esports – video game competitions – thrives through connections with OOH advertising.

YouGov conducted online interviews between May 2020 and May 2021. The U.S. data is based on a sample of more than 2,000 adults aged 18+ who responded that esports is a 'top interest' or that they are 'somewhat interested in esports'. More than 1,000 British adults aged 18+ answered the same questions in surveys conducted in Great Britain. The participants of this study were deemed to be 'avid esports fans.'

According to the study, 68 percent of American esports fans used their phones to search for goods or services after seeing them advertised on a billboard, versus 23 percent of American adults. This group is also more likely to talk about what they've seen with friends or family, especially those aged 18-34. The proportion of esports fans who noticed OOH advertising on trains was nearly the same as those who noticed ads on the internet, at 67 and 65 percent, respectively. Furthermore, ads in taxis are more noticeable to this audience than to other adult British consumers. Trust may explain this trend among esports fans. According to the YouGov survey, esports fans in the U.S. (58 percent) and Great Britain (50 percent) distrust TV ads, leaving brands and publishers to explore other ways of advertising.

It is clear that a brand can gain the attention and loyalty of sports fans by combining marketing with OOH ads. By combining place-based and contextualized media with striking graphics, a brand will capture the hearts and minds of sports fans across the globe.

Let's look at some examples of sports-driven OOH ads.

Tim Hortons, a Canadian restaurant chain known for its coffee, doughnuts and connection to Canada's national identity, used a play on words to show support and garner attention from local Toronto Maple Leafs fans. Tim Hortons' roots with the Toronto Maple Leafs run deep, since it was founded by and named for one of its all-time great players. During the first round of the team's run in this year's NHL playoffs, it offered some words of encouragement.

Ads from the quick service restaurant featured a picture of a Boston cream doughnut next to a slight rearrangement of its name that also served as a rallying cry during the Maple Leafs' series against their longtime rivals, the Boston Bruins: "Cream Boston." The ads appeared on OOH boards and in-store digital signage, as well as on social media.

Ahead of the playoff series returning home to Toronto on the following Monday, the QSR's signs were also made dark, except for the letters "T O."

A show of hometown support was also done in support of the Toronto Raptors, who were at that time also in the midst of a playoff run.

The campaign was not the first time Tim Hortons had antagonized the Boston Bruins. During the 2014 Stanley Cup Playoffs, when the Montreal Canadiens were set to face the

Boston Bruins in the second round, JWT Montreal released ads showing a bite taken out of a Boston cream donut, next to the words "Boston, on va les manger" ("Boston, we'll eat them").

Nike partnered with LeBron James in the Chinese market to capitalize on the NBA and LeBron's widespread popularity to spread a positive message around youth empowerment in sports. "This campaign was inspired by that moment, turning a call to be silenced into a platform to speak even louder," Nike said in a statement.

Wieden+Kennedy Shanghai had created the campaign in order to encourage Chinese athletes to keep following their passions, including sports. The campaign emphasized LeBron's efforts off the court, such as opening a school and starting a company. The campaign was launched with OOH in nine Chinese cities: Shanghai, Beijing, Nanjing, Chengdu, Harbin, Tianjin, Hangzhou, Chongqing and Suzhou.

Nike also installed pop-up spaces in New York City around the 348 Bowery Manhattan retail space, which served as a retail space and an introductory platform for the new Nike SNKRS app. This app provides a unique product experience and the ability to purchase sneakers seamlessly. The store hosted restocks of some very sought-after shoes, as well as early sales for pairs like the "Metallic Gold" Nike Air Foamposite One. The facade of the Nike SNKRS Station was a massive, animated display featuring a countdown clock that revealed a new sneaker to be sold at the location each day.

With the best brand awareness campaigns, now is the time to target sports audiences with DOOH to influence their purchasing decisions.

An interesting side note to OOH's influence in the sports sector is that sports betting is also seeing benefits from OOH advertising worldwide. According to the OAAA, over half (54%)

of dwellers in large (1M+) cities have recently noticed OOH ads for sports betting/gambling, compared to only a third (36%) of the general population noticing the same static advertisements. Not surprisingly, more than 3 out of 5 (62%) Americans who saw ads for sports betting engaged in some way after seeing the OOH ads, including sharing information, with word-of-mouth being the most common engagement (51%), followed by website visitation (47%).

Chapter Five

Other Pro AV Focus Areas

Role of Systems Integrators

An AV integrator's job is to oversee the needs, analysis, design, installation, components, maintenance and management of a company's Pro AV system. Their involvement is by no means a one-size-fits-all service, as every business and project is different. In fact, systems integrators are increasingly necessary as AV projects become more interactive and engaging and therefore more complex. As mass implementation of digital signage solutions continues, system managers and designers are increasingly responsible for driving business outcomes.

AV Industry

Manufacturing Companies

Audio Manufacturers

Companies primarily engaged in the development, manufacturing and distribution of audio equipment

Visual Manufacturers

Companies primarily engaged in the development, manufacturing and distribution of visual equipment

Diversified AV

Companies primarily engaged in the development, manufacturing and distribution of audiovisual equipment; often large diversified conglomerates

Sales Channels

Retailers

Direct-To-Consumer

Business-To-Business

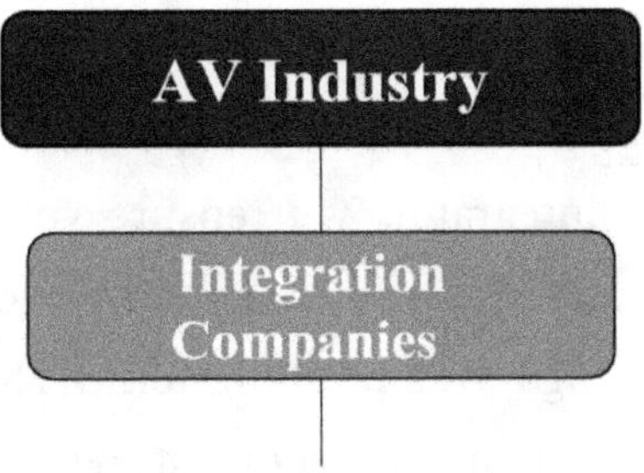

Overview

Use components from audiovisual manufacturers to create communication and presentation solutions for workplaces, higher education and events, among others

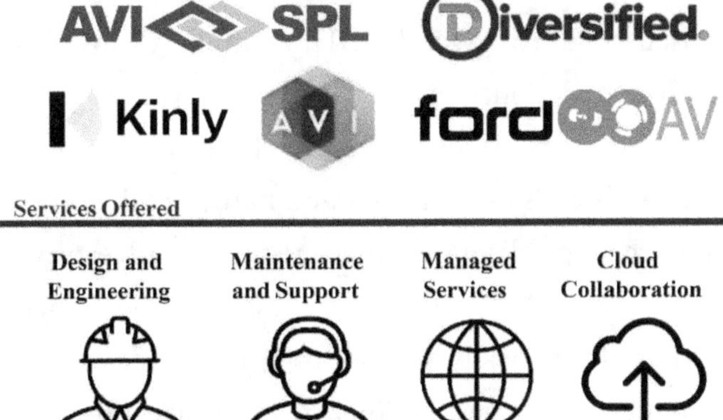

Services Offered

Source: Solomon Partners

An AV systems integrator has authority over the project and all stakeholders. Their technical prowess is often the heart of a brand's specialized campaign that attracts the most viewers. They are the person that problems escalate to, are responsible for the budget, and ensure the right people are available to work on the project.

An AV systems integrator is responsible for keeping your AV systems cost-effective and running without a hitch. In addition, by hiring an AV integrator, you ensure your AV system is designed to operate with maximum efficiency and minimal issues for cost savings over the long term. The more moving parts a project has, the more important the systems integrator role becomes.

Importance of Software, Audio and Lighting

When discussing Pro AV and OOH, we must acknowledge that lighting, sound and out of home advertising work together. For example, digital menu boards are both Pro AV and OOH. Digital menu boards use software and hardware that is Pro AV, and OOH through display digital media and advertising. The effectiveness of OOH, especially pedestrian-level signage and kiosks, rises dramatically when Pro AV is added. The older kiosk and digital signage solutions are expensive, unreliable and complex. Businesses need new technology that modernizes their experience without the difficulties involved with traditional systems.

<u>Software</u>

With the right balance of Pro AV, outdoor advertising can become modernized and integrated with the internet, opening doors to access social media, the cloud and more.

Various technological advancements, such as the integration of Pro AV with the Internet of Things (IoT) and cloud-computing systems, are creating growth. Cloud-based platforms reduce maintenance requirements and provide teams the power to remotely manage any deployed device to deliver seamless experiences. With a comprehensive, fully-integrated solution across all devices and peripherals, businesses can become leaders in digital transformation.

These Pro AV technologies are effective for live events, transportation, venues, retail, digital signage, sustainability efforts, collaboration, learning, security and surveillance. Other factors, including the development of 360-degree cameras, drones, augmented reality (AR) and virtual reality (VR) systems and improvements in telecommunication infrastructure, offer specialized content, driving the market further.

One Pro AV market challenge is educating business owners, event managers, marketing directors and executives to understand the importance of each of the Pro AV technologies.

<u>Audio</u>

In many businesses, schools and entertainment arenas, the attention and money have been primarily focused on the visual side of things. Studies show that audio recognition and clarity are equally important in getting your message understood, enhancing recognition memory.[26]

One could think of it as if they were in a theater watching an epic adventure unfold on-screen. The visuals can be compelling, but if the audience struggles to understand the dialogue, the meaning and experience's memorability is lost. If there is just enough tension to wear on the subconscious mind, the consumer will often lose interest before the entire message is relayed even if the sound is "good enough" for the dialogue to be heard.

When budgets are limited, the first thing to be reduced is often the quality of the audio. Thus, it becomes important for the client utilizing technical service to understand the value of Pro AV.

Lighting

Audio Video Lighting (AVL), which is the combination of audio and video with lighting tools, is critical to integrating a fully-immersive experience. The AVL equipment should complement the event, no more and no less. Setting the proper lighting mood requires both technical prowess and an understanding of the anticipated audience. Therefore, the

---

[26] Van Engen KJ, Chandrasekaran B, Smiljanic R (2012) Effects of Speech Clarity on Recognition Memory for Spoken Sentences.

architectural lighting industry employs lighting designers to make sure the experiential end goal is accomplished. Lighting can determine the quality of the experience in the eyes of even inexperienced viewers.

The purpose of AVL is to make an event or installation look and sound better. AV engineering consultants understand that lighting is vital to create the desired experience and atmosphere. The wrong lighting would be like walking into a day spa and finding it lit up like a sports stadium; it would ruin the relaxing experience. You can easily distract your customers with poor lighting, causing them to miss important elements or moments. Bad lighting is one of the qualities of a low-budget environment.

Advancements in the image projection segment of Pro AV are evolving rapidly. Innovations such as micro-LEDs, an LED display that uses very small pixels, greatly reduces energy requirements and has a longer lifespan than OLED panels.[27] Given the research, development and investment in the sector, we expect there will continue to be significant innovation and new technology, including screens providing a 360-degree experience for viewers.

The best AVL implementations place the message or brand front and center. Thus, it is important to understand the dynamics of a fully and professionally integrated effort.

Augmented Reality (AR) and Pro AV

Augmented Reality is an interactive experience that combines the real world with computer-generated content. AR is different from Virtual Reality in that it is not immersive. Rather, it adds a layer to the physical world. Using Pro AV, AR projects an environmental simulation to replace your world entirely. With AR, you invite the audience to be a part of the presentation. You provide them an opportunity to directly participate in and explore what you're sharing. The presentation is more compelling and engaging, and audience members feel in control

---

[27] Futuresource 2022 Global LED Display Market Report.

of their learning experience. These developments have led to the integration of AV and AR into retail environments and offices.

Early adopters in retail services have incorporated AV and AR technologies to help enhance shopping experiences for consumers, using AR to help consumers visualize different products in different environments.

An example of AR involving in-store media has visitors using their phone cameras to find enhanced content superimposed on the real world. You can visualize how new furniture or decor may look in your home before buying it.

In-store navigation can also be enhanced using AR, with applications creating pathways for customers to follow as they track specific items they are looking for within the store. This removes the hassle of guessing aisle by aisle or seeking a store representative.

Businesses are also using AR to enhance the at-home shopping experience, allowing customers to virtually "try-on clothes" in digital fitting rooms.

New OOH entertainment is also being developed using AR, including immersive art experiences, virtual museum tours and site-based gaming experiences.

Conclusion

Pro AV and OOH Media have become rapidly advancing, increasingly profitable mediums. We believe that the OOH media and advertising channel deploying Pro AV will continue to benefit from the quickly progressing technological transformations we have seen over the past few years. Those advances, combined with public acceptance of digital communication and populations interested to engage in activities outside of their homes, will fuel progress and profitability for the foreseeable future.

OOH will continue to show a considerable marketing mix penetration increase in the coming years. Keep in mind that even a few incremental marketing mix penetration percentage points from four percent to six or seven percent of overall media spend would be a massive multi-billion dollar change for the U.S. OOH industry.

Advances in mobile tech has made digital OOH advertising more accountable than ever before, using mobile phones to track consumer purchase and viewing activity for purposes of attribution. Companies can easily track, target, and reach consumers at more points throughout their day using location-based data. But the focus needs to continue to be on a consumer's journey in addition to their location. As people spend more time with digital media, the opportunities to reach consumers with digital media while they are in purchase mode will multiply.

The advertising dollar has never been so easily held accountable, so easily precisely placed, so easily maximized. Every brand today needs to co-exist in physical and digital channels.

Across the Pro AV industry we are seeing consolidation by and among the major operators. Given the substantial cost savings and revenue synergies that can be created by acquisitions, we expect large operators to pursue acquisitions aggressively.

Next Steps

We recommend attending the following industry conferences:

- Digital Signage Experience (co-located with Live Design International)
  - https://www.digitalsignageexperience.com/

- DPAA Media Summit
  - https://dpaaglobal.com/

- Infocomm
  - https://www.infocommshow.org/

- ISE
  - http://ise2023.org/

- NRF: Retail's Big Show
  - https://nrfbigshow.nrf.com/

- OAAA/Geopath
  - https://oaaa.org/

- Out Of Home New York

- World Out of Home Organization Congress
  - https://www.worldooh.org/

We recommend signing up for the following publications:

- AV Network
  - https://www.avnetwork.com/

- Billboard Insider
  - https://billboardinsider.com/

- DailyDOOH
  - http://www.dailydooh.com/

- Digital Signage Pulse
  - https://digitalsignagepulse.com/

- Sixteen:Nine
  - https://www.sixteen-nine.net/

In addition, we recommend joining the following trade associations:

- AVIXA – Audio Visual and Integrated Experience Association
- DPAA – Digital Place-based Advertising Association
- DSF – Digital Signage Federation
- OAAA – Out of home Advertising Association of America
- WOOHO – World Out Of Home Organization

Appendix

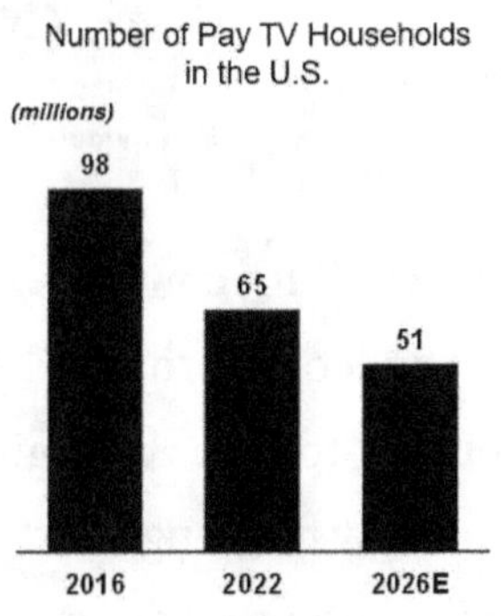

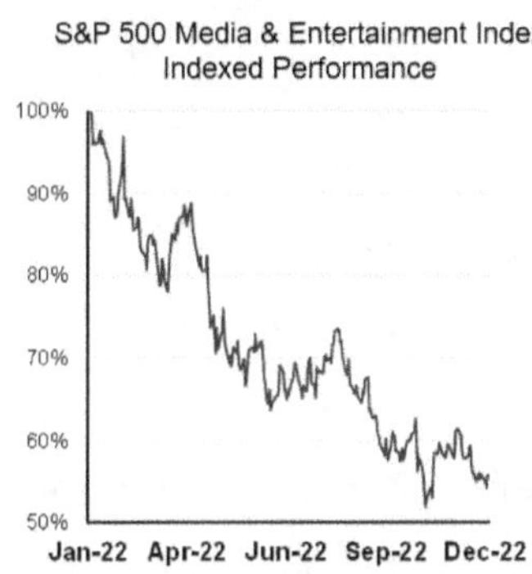

Pay TV households have declined as more people opt for less expensive and more convenient streaming services, leading to a fall in select media and entertainment stocks. Companies in the industry are struggling to adapt to the changing landscape, with some attempting to launch their own streaming services. As a result, the segment is becoming saturated, and it is increasingly difficult to attain market share. The decline in pay TV households will have a lasting impact on the overall segment.

---

[28] eMarketer, company filings and S&P Capital IQ.

<u>U.S. Advertising Market – Growth By Segment[29]</u>

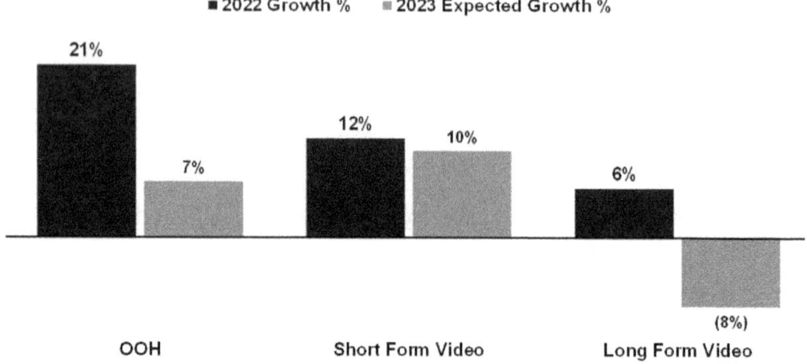

The OOH advertising industry is expected to continue its growth trend in 2023, while long form video is projected to decline. This trend could be attributed to the changing preferences of consumers who are increasingly favoring shorter-form video content over longer-form content. Advertising budgets will likely pursue alternative channels such as OOH, which has proven to be effective in capturing consumer attention and driving engagement.

---

[29] OAAA, MAGNA Global Ad Forecasts, December 2022.

<u>Media Fragmentation[30]</u>

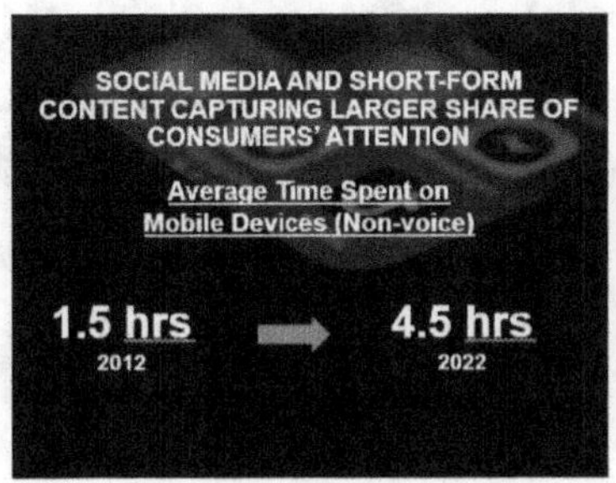

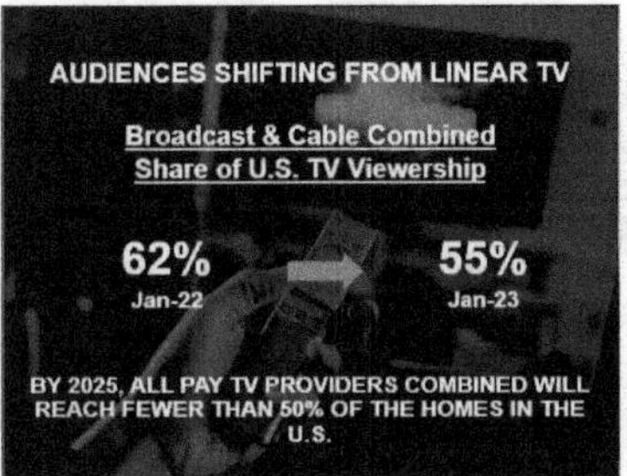

Social media and short-form content are gaining a larger share of consumers' attention, at the expense of traditional media channels such as TV, radio, and print. This trend is reflective of the changing media landscape and the shift towards mobile-first consumption habits. Additionally, audiences are shifting away from linear TV towards on-demand streaming services, signaling a fundamental change in how consumers are engaging with video content and a need for advertisers to adapt their strategies accordingly.

---

[30] eMarketer, GroupM and Nielsen.

<u>Radio and Newspaper Audiences Continue to Shrink[31]</u>

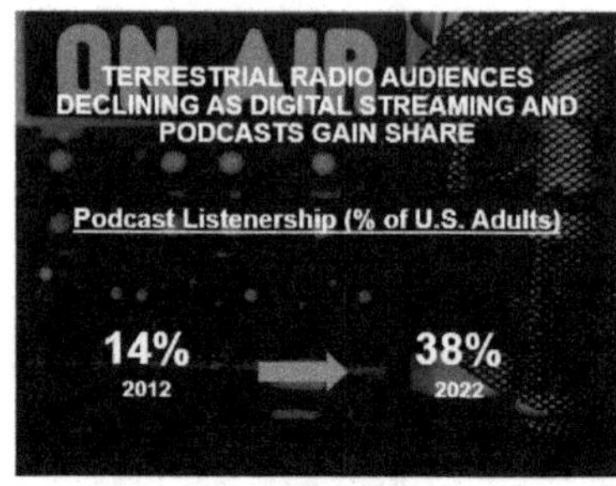

Radio and newspapers are experiencing a decrease in viewership, a trend that has been growing over the span of several years. This decline could be attributed to the rise of digital media and changing consumer habits, as more and more people turn to online platforms and social media for news and entertainment.

---

[31] Edison Research and Pew Research.

About the Author

Mark Boidman is a Partner and Global Head of Media at Solomon Partners. With more than 23 years of experience in public and private mergers, acquisitions, divestitures, leveraged financings, private placements and restructurings, Mark has advised clients in industry changing transactions with a combined value exceeding $45 billion. Mark advises companies across the media and technology sectors, including digital media and media and tech services.

He is recognized for his expertise in advertising and marketing services-based businesses, mobile, in-store media, retail tech and professional AV, event tech and out of home media. Mark's first book, *Times Square Everywhere*, analyzes how digital and mobile media are changing the media landscape.

Before joining Solomon, Mark was the head of Barclays' (originally Lehman Brothers) out of home media, TV broadcasting and radio coverage in its Global Technology, Media and Telecom Group. Prior to Lehman Brothers, Mark was an attorney in the M&A Group at Paul, Weiss, Rifkind, Wharton & Garrison.

www.ingramcontent.com/pod-product-compliance
Lightning Source LLC
Chambersburg PA
CBHW051654060726
47593CB00021B/1087